D0391568

# Blasted

## Sarah Kane

'*Blasted* is exciting and noble, both in its theatrical ideas and ambitions.' *Evening Standard*

'It is a visionary play, but its sense of reality is so meticulously and bloodcurdlingly intense that the whole play feels like a symbol: an image in action, as in Strindberg or the early expressionists.' *Sunday Times*

'Seeing the play now one is also struck by the density of its references and its strange element of hope.' *Guardian*

'Pierced with eloquent despair her writing has an arresting poetic power and a potent theme of yearning – for love or some sort of meaningful human contact which seems just beyond the reach of the characters.' *Mail on Sunday*

'Beckett's vision was metaphysical, Kane's is moral, social, political and very much of our times.' *The Times*

'Kane . . . had genuine artistic vision and great dramatic talent.' *Daily Telegraph*

**Sarah Kane** was born in 1971. Her first play *Blasted* was produced at the Royal Court Theatre Upstairs in 1995. Her second play, *Phaedra's Love*, was produced at the Gate Theatre in 1996. In April 1998, *Cleansed* was produced at the Royal Court Theatre Downstairs and in September 1998, *Crave* was produced by Paines Plough and Bright Ltd at the Traverse Theatre, Edinburgh. Her last play, *4.48 Psychosis*, premiered at the Royal Court Jerwood Theatre Upstairs in June 2000. Her short film *Skin*, produced by British Screen/Channel Four, premiered in June 1997. Sarah Kane died in 1999.

# Blasted

*For Vincent O'Connell, with thanks.*

*methuen* | drama

LONDON · NEW YORK · OXFORD · NEW DELHI · SYDNEY

METHUEN DRAMA
Bloomsbury Publishing Plc
50 Bedford Square, London, WC1B 3DP, UK
1385 Broadway, New York, NY 10018, USA

BLOOMSBURY, METHUEN DRAMA and the Methuen Drama logo are
trademarks of Bloomsbury Publishing Plc

*Blasted* first published in 1995 by Methuen in *Frontline Intelligence 2*,
This edition first published in Great Britain in 2002 by Methuen Publishing Ltd
Reprinted by Bloomsbury Methuen Drama 2009 (twice), 2010, 2012, 2014, 2015 (twice),
2016, 2017, 2018

© Sarah Kane 1995

Sarah Kane has asserted her right under the Copyright, Designs and Patents Act, 1988, to be
identified as author of this work.

All rights reserved. No part of this publication may be reproduced or transmitted in any form or
by any means, electronic or mechanical, including photocopying, recording, or any information
storage or retrieval system, without prior permission in writing from the publishers.

Bloomsbury Publishing Plc does not have any control over, or responsibility for, any third-party
websites referred to or in this book. All internet addresses given in this book were correct at the
time of going to press. The author and publisher regret any inconvenience caused if addresses have
changed or sites have ceased to exist, but can accept no responsibility for any such changes.

No rights in incidental music or songs contained in the work are hereby granted and
performance rights for any performance/presentation whatsoever must be obtained from
the respective copyright owners.

All rights whatsoever in this play are strictly reserved and application for performance etc. should
be made before rehearsals by professionals and by amateurs to Casarotto Ramsay & Associates
Ltd, Waverley House, 7–12 Noel Street, London W1F 8GQ Mail to: agents@casarotto.co.uk.
No performance may be given unless a licence has been obtained.

A catalogue record for this book is available from the British Library.

ISBN: PB: 978-0-4137-6620-5

A catalog record for this book is available from the Library of Congress.

Series: Modern Plays

Typeset by Delatype Ltd, Birkenhead
Printed and bound in Great Britain

To find out more about our authors and books visit www.bloomsbury.com
and sign up for our newsletters.

*Blasted* was first performed at the Royal Court Theatre Upstairs, London, on 12 January 1995. The cast was as follows:

| | |
|---|---|
| **Ian** | Pip Donaghy |
| **Cate** | Kate Ashfield |
| **Soldier** | Dermot Kerrigan |

*Directed by* James Macdonald
*Designed by* Franziska Wilcken
*Lighting by* Jon Linstrum
*Sound by* Paul Arditti

## Characters

**Ian**
**Cate**
**Soldier**

## Author's note

Punctuation is used to indicate delivery, not to conform to the rules of grammar.

A stroke (/) marks the point of interruption in overlapping dialogue.

Words in square brackets [ ] are not spoken, but have been included in the text to clarify meaning.

Stage directions in brackets ( ) function as lines.

## Editor's note

This edition of *Blasted*, first reprinted in 2000, incorporates minor revisions made to the original text by Sarah Kane shortly before her death. It should therefore be regarded as the definitive version in all respects.

## Scene One

*A very expensive hotel room in Leeds – the kind that is so expensive it could be anywhere in the world.*

*There is a large double bed.*
*A mini-bar and champagne on ice.*
*A telephone.*
*A large bouquet of flowers.*
*Two doors – one is the entrance from the corridor, the other leads off to the bathroom.*

*Two people enter –* **Ian** *and* **Cate**.

**Ian** *is 45, Welsh born but lived in Leeds much of his life and picked up the accent.*

**Cate** *is 21, a lower-middle-class Southerner with a south London accent and a stutter when under stress.*

*They enter.*

**Cate** *stops at the door, amazed at the classiness of the room.*
**Ian** *comes in, throws a small pile of newspapers on the bed, goes straight to the mini-bar and pours himself a large gin.*
*He looks briefly out of the window at the street, then turns back to the room.*

**Ian**  I've shat in better places than this.

(*He gulps down the gin.*)

I stink.
You want a bath?

**Cate**  (*Shakes her head.*)

**Ian** *goes into the bathroom and we hear him run the water. He comes back in with only a towel around his waist and a revolver in his hand. He checks it is loaded and puts it under his pillow.*

**Ian**  Tip that wog when he brings up the sandwiches.

*He leaves fifty pence and goes into the bathroom.*
*Cate comes further into the room.*
*She puts her bag down and bounces on the bed.*
*She goes around the room, looking in every drawer, touching everything.*
*She smells the flowers and smiles.*

**Cate**   Lovely.

*Ian comes back in, hair wet, towel around his waist, drying himself off.*
*He stops and looks at Cate who is sucking her thumb.*
*He goes back in the bathroom where he dresses.*
*We hear him coughing terribly in the bathroom.*
*He spits in the sink and re-enters.*

**Cate**   You all right?

**Ian**   It's nothing.

*He pours himself another gin, this time with ice and tonic, and sips it at a more normal pace.*
*He collects his gun and puts it in his under-arm holster.*
*He smiles at Cate.*

**Ian**   I'm glad you've come. Didn't think you would.

   (*He offers her champagne.*)

**Cate**   (*Shakes her head.*)

   I was worried.

**Ian**   This? (*He indicates his chest.*) Don't matter.

**Cate**   I didn't mean that. You sounded unhappy.

**Ian**   (*Pops the champagne. He pours them both a glass.*)

**Cate**   What we celebrating?

**Ian**   (*Doesn't answer. He goes to the window and looks out.*)

   Hate this city. Stinks. Wogs and Pakis taking over.

**Cate**   You shouldn't call them that.

**Ian**    Why not?

**Cate**    It's not very nice.

**Ian**    You a nigger-lover?

**Cate**    Ian, don't.

**Ian**    You like our coloured brethren?

**Cate**    Don't mind them.

**Ian**    Grow up.

**Cate**    There's Indians at the day centre where my brother goes. They're really polite.

**Ian**    So they should be.

**Cate**    He's friends with some of them.

**Ian**    Retard, isn't he?

**Cate**    No, he's got learning difficulties.

**Ian**    Aye. Spaz.

**Cate**    No he's not.

**Ian**    Glad my son's not a Joey.

**Cate**    Don't c- call him that.

**Ian**    Your mother I feel sorry for. Two of you like it.

**Cate**    Like wh- what?

**Ian**    (*Looks at her, deciding whether or not to continue. He decides against it.*)

    You know I love you.

**Cate**    (*Smiles a big smile, friendly and non-sexual.*)

**Ian**    Don't want you ever to leave.

**Cate**    I'm here for the night.

**Ian**   (*Drinks.*)

Sweating again. Stink. You ever thought of getting married?

**Cate**   Who'd marry me?

**Ian**   I would.

**Cate**   I couldn't.

**Ian**   You don't love me. I don't blame you, I wouldn't.

**Cate**   I couldn't leave Mum.

**Ian**   Have to one day.

**Cate**   Why?

**Ian**   (*Opens his mouth to answer but can't think of one.*)

*There is a knock at the door.*
**Ian** *starts, and* **Cate** *goes to answer it.*

**Ian**   Don't.

**Cate**   Why not?

**Ian**   I said.

*He takes his gun from the holster and goes to the door.*
*He listens.*
*Nothing.*

**Cate**   (*Giggles.*)

**Ian**   Shh.

*He listens.*
*Still nothing.*

**Ian**   Probably the wog with the sarnies. Open it.

**Cate** *opens the door.*
*There's no one there, just a tray of sandwiches on the floor.*
*She brings them in and examines them.*

**Cate**   Ham. Don't believe it.

**Ian**    (*Takes a sandwich and eats it.*)

Champagne?

**Cate**    (*Shakes her head.*)

**Ian**    Got something against ham?

**Cate**    Dead meat. Blood. Can't eat an animal.

**Ian**    No one would know.

**Cate**    No, I can't, I actually can't, I'd puke all over the place.

**Ian**    It's only a pig.

**Cate**    I'm hungry.

**Ian**    Have one of these.

**Cate**    I CAN'T.

**Ian**    I'll take you out for an Indian.
Jesus, what's this? Cheese.

> **Cate** *beams.*
> *She separates the cheese sandwiches from the ham ones, and eats.*
> **Ian** *watches her.*

**Ian**    Don't like your clothes.

**Cate**    (*Looks down at her clothes.*)

**Ian**    You look like a lesbos.

**Cate**    What's that?

**Ian**    Don't look very sexy, that's all.

**Cate**    Oh.

(*She continues to eat.*)

Don't like your clothes either.

**Ian**    (*Looks down at his clothes.*
*Then gets up, takes them all off and stands in front of her, naked.*)

Put your mouth on me.

**Cate** (*Stares. Then bursts out laughing.*)

**Ian** No?
Fine.
Because I stink?

**Cate** (*Laughs even more.*)

> **Ian** *attempts to dress, but fumbles with embarrassment.*
> *He gathers his clothes and goes into the bathroom where he dresses.*
> **Cate** *eats, and giggles over the sandwiches.*
> **Ian** *returns, fully dressed.*
> *He picks up his gun, unloads and reloads it.*

**Ian** You got a job yet?

**Cate** No.

**Ian** Still screwing the taxpayer.

**Cate** Mum gives me money.

**Ian** When are you going to stand on your own feet?

**Cate** I've applied for a job at an advertising agency.

**Ian** (*Laughs genuinely.*)

No chance.

**Cate** Why not?

**Ian** (*Stops laughing and looks at her.*)

Cate. You're stupid. You're never going to get a job.

**Cate** I am. I am not.

**Ian** See.

**Cate** St- Stop it. You're doing it deliberately.

**Ian** Doing what?

**Cate** C- Confusing me.

**Ian** No, I'm talking, you're just too thick to understand.

**Cate**    I am not, I am not.

> **Cate** *begins to tremble.* **Ian** *is laughing.*
> **Cate** *faints.*
> **Ian** *stops laughing and stares at her motionless body.*

**Ian**    Cate?

> (*He turns her over and lifts up her eyelids.*
> *He doesn't know what to do.*
> *He gets a glass of gin and dabs some on her face.*)

**Cate**    (*Sits bolt upright, eyes open but still unconscious.*)

**Ian**    Fucking Jesus.

**Cate**    (*Bursts out laughing, unnaturally, hysterically, uncontrollably.*)

**Ian**    Stop fucking about.

**Cate**    (*Collapses again and lies still.*)

> **Ian** *stands by helplessly.*
> *After a few moments,* **Cate** *comes round as if waking up in the morning.*

**Ian**    What the Christ was that?

**Cate**    Have to tell her.

**Ian**    Cate?

**Cate**    She's in danger.

> (*She closes her eyes and slowly comes back to normal.*
> *She looks at* **Ian** *and smiles.*)

**Ian**    What now?

**Cate**    Did I faint?

**Ian**    That was real?

**Cate**    Happens all the time.

**Ian**    What, fits?

**Cate**  Since Dad came back.

**Ian**  Does it hurt?

**Cate**  I'll grow out of it the doctor says.

**Ian**  How do you feel?

**Cate**  (*Smiles.*)

**Ian**  Thought you were dead.

**Cate**  [I] Suppose that's what it's like.

**Ian**  Don't do it again, fucking scared me.

**Cate**  Don't know much about it, I just go. Feels like I'm away for minutes or months sometimes, then I come back just where I was.

**Ian**  It's terrible.

**Cate**  I didn't go far.

**Ian**  What if you didn't come round?

**Cate**  Wouldn't know. I'd stay there.

**Ian**  Can't stand it.

(*He goes to the mini-bar and pours himself another large gin and lights a cigarette.*)

**Cate**  What?

**Ian**  Death. Not being.

**Cate**  You fall asleep and then you wake up.

**Ian**  How do you know?

**Cate**  Why don't you give up smoking?

**Ian**  (*Laughs.*)

**Cate**  You should. They'll make you ill.

**Ian**  Too late for that.

**Cate**   Whenever I think of you it's with a cigarette and a gin.

**Ian**   Good.

**Cate**   They make your clothes smell.

**Ian**   Don't forget my breath.

**Cate**   Imagine what your lungs must look like.

**Ian**   Don't need to imagine. I've seen.

**Cate**   When?

**Ian**   Last year. When I came round, surgeon brought in this lump of rotting pork, stank. My lung.

**Cate**   He took it out?

**Ian**   Other one's the same now.

**Cate**   But you'll die.

**Ian**   Aye.

**Cate**   Please stop smoking.

**Ian**   Won't make any difference.

**Cate**   Can't they do something?

**Ian**   No. It's not like your brother, look after him he'll be all right.

**Cate**   They die young.

**Ian**   I'm fucked.

**Cate**   Can't you get a transplant?

**Ian**   Don't be stupid. They give them to people with a life. Kids.

**Cate**   People die in accidents all the time, they must have some spare.

**Ian**   Why? What for? Keep me alive to die of cirrhosis in three months' time.

**Cate**   You're making it worse, speeding it up.

**Ian**   Enjoy myself while I'm here.

(*He inhales deeply on his cigarette and swallows the last of the gin neat.*)

[I'll] Call that coon, get some more sent up.

**Cate**   (*Shakes.*)

**Ian**   Wonder if the conker understands English.

*He notices* **Cate**'s *distress and cuddles her.*
*He kisses her.*
*She pulls away and wipes her mouth.*

**Cate**   Don't put your tongue in, I don't like it.

**Ian**   Sorry.

*The telephone rings loudly.* **Ian** *starts, then answers it.*

**Ian**   Hello?

**Cate**   Who is it?

**Ian**   (*Covers the mouthpiece.*) Shh.

(*Into the mouthpiece.*) Got it here.

(*He takes a notebook from the pile of newspapers and dictates down the phone.*)

A serial killer slaughtered British tourist Samantha Scrace, S – C – R – A – C – E, in a sick murder ritual comma, police revealed yesterday point new par. The bubbly nineteen year old from Leeds was among seven victims found buried in identical triangular tombs in an isolated New Zealand forest point new par. Each had been stabbed more than twenty times and placed face down comma, hands bound behind their backs point new par. Caps up, ashes at the site showed the maniac had stayed to cook a meal, caps down point new par. Samantha comma, a beautiful redhead with dreams of becoming a model comma, was on the trip of a lifetime after finishing her A levels last year point. Samantha's heartbroken mum said yesterday colon quoting, we pray the police will come up with something dash, anything comma, soon point still quoting. The sooner this lunatic is brought to justice the better point end quote new par. The Foreign Office warned tourists Down Under to take extra care point. A spokesman said colon quoting, common sense is the best rule point end quote, copy ends.

(*He listens. Then he laughs.*)

Exactly.

(*He listens.*)

That one again, I went to see her. Scouse tart, spread her legs. No. Forget it. Tears and lies, not worth the space.

(*He presses a button on the phone to connect him to room service.*)

Tosser.

**Cate**  How do they know you're here?

**Ian**  Told them.

**Cate**  Why?

**Ian**  In case they needed me.

**Cate**  Silly. We came here to be away from them.

**Ian**  Thought you'd like this. Nice hotel.

(*Into the mouthpiece.*)

Bring a bottle of gin up, son.

(*He puts the phone down.*)

**Cate**  We always used to go to yours.

**Ian**  That was years ago. You've grown up.

**Cate**   (*Smiles.*)

**Ian**   I'm not well any more.

**Cate**   (*Stops smiling.*)

> **Ian** *kisses her.*
> *She responds.*
> *He puts his hand under her top and moves it towards her breast.*
> *With the other hand he undoes his trousers and starts masturbating.*
> *He begins to undo her top.*
> *She pushes him away.*

**Cate**   Ian, d- don't.

**Ian**   What?

**Cate**   I don't w- want to do this.

**Ian**   Yes you do.

**Cate**   I don't.

**Ian**   Why not? You're nervous, that's all.

> (*He starts to kiss her again.*)

**Cate**   I t- t- t- t- t- t- t- told you. I really like you but I
c- c- c- c- can't do this.

**Ian**   (*Kissing her.*) Shhh.

> (*He starts to undo her trousers.*)

> **Cate** *panics.*
> *She starts to tremble and make inarticulate crying sounds.*
> **Ian** *stops, frightened of bringing another 'fit' on.*

**Ian**   All right, Cate, it's all right. We don't have to do
anything.

> *He strokes her face until she has calmed down.*
> *She sucks her thumb.*
> *Then.*

**Ian**   That wasn't very fair.

**Cate**  What?

**Ian**  Leaving me hanging, making a prick of myself.

**Cate**  I f- f- felt –

**Ian**  Don't pity me, Cate. You don't have to fuck me 'cause I'm dying, but don't push your cunt in my face then take it away 'cause I stick my tongue out.

**Cate**  I- I- Ian.

**Ian**  What's the m- m- matter?

**Cate**  I k- k- kissed you, that's all. I l- l- like you.

**Ian**  Don't give me a hard-on if you're not going to finish me off. It hurts.

**Cate**  I'm sorry.

**Ian**  Can't switch it on and off like that. If I don't come my cock aches.

**Cate**  I didn't mean it.

**Ian**  Shit. (*He appears to be in considerable pain.*)

**Cate**  I'm sorry. I am. I won't do it again.

> **Ian**, *apparently still in pain, takes her hand and grasps it around his penis, keeping his own hand over the top.*
> *Like this, he masturbates until he comes with some genuine pain.*
> *He releases* **Cate***'s hand and she withdraws it.*

**Cate**  Is it better?

**Ian**  (*Nods.*)

**Cate**  I'm sorry.

**Ian**  Don't worry. Can we make love tonight?

**Cate**  No.

**Ian**  Why not?

**Cate**  I'm not your girlfriend any more.

**Ian**   Will you be my girlfriend again?

**Cate**   I can't.

**Ian**   Why not?

**Cate**   I told Shaun I'd be his.

**Ian**   Have you slept with him?

**Cate**   No.

**Ian**   Slept with me before. You're more mine than his.

**Cate**   I'm not.

**Ian**   What was that about then, wanking me off?

**Cate**   I d- d- d- d-

**Ian**   Sorry. Pressure, pressure. I love you, that's all.

**Cate**   You were horrible to me.

**Ian**   I wasn't.

**Cate**   Stopped phoning me, never said why.

**Ian**   It was difficult, Cate.

**Cate**   Because I haven't got a job?

**Ian**   No, pet, not that.

**Cate**   Because of my brother?

**Ian**   No, no, Cate. Leave it now.

**Cate**   That's not fair.

**Ian**   I said leave it.

(*He reaches for his gun.*)

*There is a knock at the door.*
**Ian** *starts, then goes to answer it.*

**Ian**   I'm not going to hurt you, just leave it. And keep quiet.
It'll only be Sooty after something.

**Cate**  Andrew.

**Ian**  What do you want to know a conker's name for?

**Cate**  I thought he was nice.

**Ian**  After a bit of black meat, eh? Won't do it with me but you'll go with a whodat.

**Cate**  You're horrible.

**Ian**  Cate, love, I'm trying to look after you. Stop you getting hurt.

**Cate**  You hurt me.

**Ian**  No, I love you.

**Cate**  Stopped loving me.

**Ian**  I've told you to leave that.
Now.

*He kisses her passionately, then goes to the door.*
*When his back is turned,* **Cate** *wipes her mouth.*
**Ian** *opens the door. There is a bottle of gin outside on a tray.*
**Ian** *brings it in and stands, unable to decide between gin and champagne.*

**Cate**  Have champagne, better for you.

**Ian**  Don't want it better for me.

*(He pours himself a gin.)*

**Cate**  You'll die quicker.

**Ian**  Thanks. Don't it scare you?

**Cate**  What?

**Ian**  Death.

**Cate**  Whose?

**Ian**  Yours.

**Cate**    Only for Mum. She'd be unhappy if I died. And my brother.

**Ian**    You're young.
When I was your age –
Now.

**Cate**    Will you have to go to hospital?

**Ian**    Nothing they can do.

**Cate**    Does Stella know?

**Ian**    What would I want to tell her for?

**Cate**    You were married.

**Ian**    So?

**Cate**    She'd want to know.

**Ian**    So she can throw a party at the coven.

**Cate**    She wouldn't do that. What about Matthew?

**Ian**    What about Matthew?

**Cate**    Have you told him?

**Ian**    I'll send him an invite for the funeral.

**Cate**    He'll be upset.

**Ian**    He hates me.

**Cate**    He doesn't.

**Ian**    He fucking does.

**Cate**    Are you upset?

**Ian**    Yes. His mother's a lesbos. Am I not preferable to that?

**Cate**    Perhaps she's a nice person.

**Ian**    She don't carry a gun.

**Cate**    I expect that's it.

**Ian**   I loved Stella till she became a witch and fucked off with a dyke, and I love you, though you've got the potential.

**Cate**   For what?

**Ian**   Sucking gash.

**Cate**   (*Utters an inarticulate sound.*)

**Ian**   You ever had a fuck with a woman?

**Cate**   No.

**Ian**   You want to?

**Cate**   Don't think so. Have you? With a man.

**Ian**   You think I'm a cocksucker? You've seen me. (*He vaguely indicates his groin.*) How can you think that?

**Cate**   I don't. I asked. You asked me.

**Ian**   You dress like a lesbos. I don't dress like a cocksucker.

**Cate**   What do they dress like?

**Ian**   Hitler was wrong about the Jews who have they hurt the queers he should have gone for scum them and the wogs and fucking football fans send a bomber over Elland Road finish them off.

(*He pours champagne and toasts the idea.*)

**Cate**   I like football.

**Ian**   Why?

**Cate**   It's good.

**Ian**   And when was the last time you went to a football match?

**Cate**   Saturday. United beat Liverpool 2–0.

**Ian**   Didn't you get stabbed?

**Cate**   Why should I?

**Ian**  That's what football's about. It's not fancy footwork and scoring goals. It's tribalism.

**Cate**  I like it.

**Ian**  You would. About your level.

**Cate**  I go to Elland Road sometimes. Would you bomb me?

**Ian**  What do you want to ask a question like that for?

**Cate**  Would you though?

**Ian**  Don't be thick.

**Cate**  But would you?

**Ian**  Haven't got a bomber.

**Cate**  Shoot me, then. Could you do that?

**Ian**  Cate.

**Cate**  Do you think it's hard to shoot someone?

**Ian**  Easy as shitting blood.

**Cate**  Could you shoot me?

**Ian**  Could you shoot me stop asking that could you shoot me you could shoot me.

**Cate**  I don't think so.

**Ian**  If I hurt you.

**Cate**  Don't think you would.

**Ian**  But if.

**Cate**  No, you're soft.

**Ian**  With people I love.

(*He stares at her, considering making a pass.*)

**Cate**  (*Smiles at him, friendly.*)

**Ian**  What's this job, then?

**Cate**  Personal Assistant.

**Ian**  Who to?

**Cate**  Don't know.

**Ian**  Who did you write the letter to?

**Cate**  Sir or madam.

**Ian**  You have to know who you're writing to.

**Cate**  It didn't say.

**Ian**  How much?

**Cate**  What?

**Ian**  Money. How much do you get paid.

**Cate**  Mum said it was a lot. I don't mind about that as long as I can go out sometimes.

**Ian**  Don't despise money. You got it easy.

**Cate**  I haven't got any money.

**Ian**  No and you haven't got kids to bring up neither.

**Cate**  Not yet.

**Ian**  Don't even think about it. Who would have children. You have kids, they grow up, they hate you and you die.

**Cate**  I don't hate Mum.

**Ian**  You still need her.

**Cate**  You think I'm stupid. I'm not stupid.

**Ian**  I worry.

**Cate**  Can look after myself.

**Ian**  Like me.

**Cate**  No.

**Ian**  You hate me, don't you.

**Cate**   You shouldn't have that gun.

**Ian**   May need it.

**Cate**   What for?

**Ian**   (*Drinks.*)

**Cate**   Can't imagine it.

**Ian**   What?

**Cate**   You. Shooting someone. You wouldn't kill anything.

**Ian**   (*Drinks.*)

**Cate**   Have you ever shot anyone?

**Ian**   Your mind.

**Cate**   Have you though?

**Ian**   Leave it now, Cate.

*She takes the warning.*
**Ian** *kisses her and lights a cigarette.*

**Ian**   When I'm with you I can't think about anything else.
You take me to another place.

**Cate**   It's like that when I have a fit.

**Ian**   Just you.

**Cate**   The world don't exist, not like this.
Looks the same but –
Time slows down.
A dream I get stuck in, can't do nothing about it.
One time –

**Ian**   Make love to me.

**Cate**   Blocks out everything else.
Once –

**Ian**   [I'll] Make love to you.

**Cate**   It's like that when I touch myself.

**Ian** *is embarrassed.*

**Cate**  Just before I'm wondering what it'll be like, and just after I'm thinking about the next one, but just as it happens it's lovely, I don't think of nothing else.

**Ian**  Like the first cigarette of the day.

**Cate**  That's bad for you though.

**Ian**  Stop talking now, you don't know anything about it.

**Cate**  Don't need to.

**Ian**  Don't know nothing. That's why I love you, want to make love to you.

**Cate**  But you can't.

**Ian**  Why not?

**Cate**  I don't want to.

**Ian**  Why did you come here?

**Cate**  You sounded unhappy.

**Ian**  Make me happy.

**Cate**  I can't.

**Ian**  Please.

**Cate**  No.

**Ian**  Why not?

**Cate**  Can't.

**Ian**  Can.

**Cate**  How?

**Ian**  You know.

**Cate**  Don't.

**Ian**  Please.

**Cate**  No.

**Ian**   I love you.

**Cate**   I don't love you.

**Ian**   (*Turns away. He sees the bouquet of flowers and picks it up.*)

These are for you.

*Blackout.*

*The sound of spring rain.*


## Scene Two

*The same.*

*Very early the following morning.*
*Bright and sunny – it's going to be a very hot day.*
*The bouquet of flowers is now ripped apart and scattered around the room.*

**Cate** *is still asleep.*
**Ian** *is awake, glancing through the newspapers.*

**Ian** *goes to the mini-bar. It is empty.*
*He finds the bottle of gin under the bed and pours half of what is left into a glass.*
*He stands looking out of the window at the street.*
*He takes the first sip and is overcome with pain.*
*He waits for it to pass, but it doesn't. It gets worse.*
**Ian** *clutches his side – it becomes extreme.*
*He begins to cough and experiences intense pain in his chest, each cough tearing at his lung.*

**Cate** *wakes and watches* **Ian**.

**Ian** *drops to his knees, puts the glass down carefully, and gives in to the pain.*
*It looks very much as if he is dying.*
*His heart, lung, liver and kidneys are all under attack and he is making involuntary crying sounds.*

*Just at the moment when it seems he cannot survive this, it begins to ease.*
*Very slowly, the pain decreases until it has all gone.*

**Ian** *is a crumpled heap on the floor.*

*He looks up and sees* **Cate** *watching him.*

**Cate**    Cunt.

**Ian**    (*Gets up slowly, picks up the glass and drinks.*
*He lights his first cigarette of the day.*)

I'm having a shower.

**Cate**    It's only six o'clock.

**Ian**    Want one?

**Cate**    Not with you.

**Ian**    Suit yourself. Cigarette?

**Cate**    (*Makes a noise of disgust.*)

*They are silent.*

**Ian** *stands, smoking and drinking neat gin.*
*When he's sufficiently numbed, he comes and goes between the bedroom and bathroom, undressing and collecting discarded towels.*
*He stops, towel around his waist, gun in hand, and looks at* **Cate**.
*She is staring at him with hate.*

**Ian**    Don't worry, I'll be dead soon.

(*He tosses the gun onto the bed.*)

Have a pop.

**Cate** *doesn't move.*
**Ian** *waits, then chuckles and goes into the bathroom.*
*We hear the shower running.*

**Cate** *stares at the gun.*
*She gets up very slowly and dresses.*
*She packs her bag.*
*She picks up* **Ian**'s *leather jacket and smells it.*

*She rips the arms off at the seams.*
*She picks up his gun and examines it.*
*We hear* **Ian** *coughing up in the bathroom.*
**Cate** *puts the gun down and he comes in.*
*He dresses.*
*He looks at the gun.*

**Ian**   No?

(*He chuckles, unloads and reloads the gun and tucks it in his holster.*)

We're one, yes?

**Cate**   (*Sneers.*)

**Ian**   We're one.
Coming down for breakfast? It's paid for.

**Cate**   Choke on it.

**Ian**   Sarky little tart this morning, aren't we?

*He picks up his jacket and puts one arm through a hole.*
*He stares at the damage, then looks at* **Cate**.
*A beat, then she goes for him, slapping him around the head hard and fast.*
*He wrestles her onto the bed, her still kicking, punching and biting.*
*She takes the gun from his holster and points it at his groin.*
*He backs off rapidly.*

**Ian**   Easy, easy, that's a loaded gun.

**Cate**   I d- d- d- d- d- d- d- d- d-

**Ian**   Catie, come on.

**Cate**   d- d- d- d- d- d- d- d- d- d-

**Ian**   You don't want an accident. Think about your mum.
And your brother. What would they think?

**Cate**   I d- d- d- d- d- d- d- d- d- d- d- d- d-

**Cate** *trembles and starts gasping for air.*
*She faints.*

**Ian** *goes to her, takes the gun and puts it back in the holster.*
*Then lies her on the bed on her back.*
*He puts the gun to her head, lies between her legs, and simulates sex.*
*As he comes,* **Cate** *sits bolt upright with a shout.*
**Ian** *moves away, unsure what to do, pointing the gun at her from behind.*
*She laughs hysterically, as before, but doesn't stop.*
*She laughs and laughs and laughs until she isn't laughing any more, she's crying her heart out.*
*She collapses again and lies still.*

**Ian**   Cate? Catie?

   **Ian** *puts the gun away.*
   *He kisses her and she comes round.*
   *She stares at him.*

**Ian**   You back?

**Cate**   Liar.

   **Ian** *doesn't know if this means yes or no, so he just waits.*
   **Cate** *closes her eyes for a few seconds, then opens them.*

**Ian**   Cate?

**Cate**   Want to go home now.

**Ian** .   It's not even seven. There won't be a train.

**Cate**   I'll wait at the station.

**Ian**   It's raining.

**Cate**   It's not.

**Ian**   Want you to stay here. Till after breakfast at least.

**Cate**   No.

**Ian**   Cate. After breakfast.

**Cate**   No.

**Ian**   (*Locks the door and pockets the key.*)

   I love you.

**Cate**   I don't want to stay.

**Ian**   Please.

**Cate**   Don't want to.

**Ian**   You make me feel safe.

**Cate**   Nothing to be scared of.

**Ian**   I'll order breakfast.

**Cate**   Not hungry.

**Ian**   (*Lights a cigarette.*)

**Cate**   How can you smoke on an empty stomach?

**Ian**   It's not empty. There's gin in it.

**Cate**   Why can't I go home?

**Ian**   (*Thinks.*)

It's too dangerous.

*Outside, a car backfires – there is an enormous bang.*
**Ian** *throws himself flat on the floor.*

**Cate**   (*Laughs.*)

It's only a car.

**Ian**   You. You're fucking thick.

**Cate**   I'm not. You're scared of things when there's nothing to be scared of. What's thick about not being scared of cars?

**Ian**   I'm not scared of cars. I'm scared of dying.

**Cate**   A car won't kill you. Not from out there.
Not unless you ran out in front of it.

(*She kisses him.*)

What's scaring you?

**Ian**   Thought it was a gun.

**Cate**    (*Kisses his neck.*)

Who'd have a gun?

**Ian**    Me.

**Cate**    (*Undoes his shirt.*)

You're in here.

**Ian**    Someone like me.

**Cate**    (*Kisses his chest.*)

Why would they shoot at you?

**Ian**    Revenge.

**Cate**    (*Runs her hands down his back.*)

**Ian**    For things I've done.

**Cate**    (*Massages his neck.*)

Tell me.

**Ian**    Tapped my phone.

**Cate**    (*Kisses the back of his neck.*)

**Ian**    Talk to people and I know I'm being listened to. I'm
sorry I stopped calling you but –

**Cate**    (*Strokes his stomach and kisses between his shoulder blades.*)

**Ian**    Got angry when you said you loved me, talking soft on
the phone, people listening to that.

**Cate**    (*Kisses his back.*)

Tell me.

**Ian**    In before you know it.

**Cate**    (*Licks his back.*)

**Ian**    Signed the Official Secrets Act, shouldn't be telling you
this.

**Cate**    (*Claws and scratches his back.*)

**Ian**    Don't want to get you into trouble.

**Cate**    (*Bites his back.*)

**Ian**    Think they're trying to kill me. Served my purpose.

**Cate**    (*Pushes him onto his back.*)

**Ian**    Done the jobs they asked. Because I love this land.

**Cate**    (*Sucks his nipples.*)

**Ian**    Stood at stations, listened to conversations and given the nod.

**Cate**    (*Undoes his trousers.*)

**Ian**    Driving jobs. Picking people up, disposing of bodies, the lot.

**Cate**    (*Begins to perform oral sex on* **Ian**.)

**Ian**    Said you were dangerous.

So I stopped.

Didn't want you in any danger.

But

Had to call you again

Missed

This

Now

I do

The real job

I

Am

A

Killer

*On the word 'killer' he comes.*
*As soon as* **Cate** *hears the word she bites his penis as hard as she can.*
**Ian***'s cry of pleasure turns into a scream of pain.*
*He tries to pull away but* **Cate** *holds on with her teeth.*
*He hits her and she lets go.*
**Ian** *lies in pain, unable to speak.*
**Cate** *spits frantically, trying to get every trace of him out of her mouth.*
*She goes to the bathroom and we hear her cleaning her teeth.*
**Ian** *examines himself. He is still in one piece.*
**Cate** *returns.*

**Cate**   You should resign.

**Ian**   Don't work like that.

**Cate**   Will they come here?

**Ian**   I don't know.

**Cate**   (*Begins to panic.*)

**Ian**   Don't start that again.

**Cate**   I c- c- c- c- c-

**Ian**   Cate, I'll shoot you myself you don't stop.
I told you because I love you, not to scare you.

**Cate**   You don't.

**Ian**   Don't argue I do. And you love me.

**Cate**   No more.

**Ian**   Loved me last night.

**Cate**   I didn't want to do it.

**Ian**   Thought you liked that.

**Cate**   No.

**Ian**   Made enough noise.

**Cate**   It was hurting.

**Ian**   Went down on Stella all the time, didn't hurt her.

**Cate**   You bit me. It's still bleeding.

**Ian**   Is that what this is all about?

**Cate**   You're cruel.

**Ian**   Don't be stupid.

**Cate**   Stop calling me that.

**Ian**   You sleep with someone holding hands and kissing you wank me off then say we can't fuck get into bed but don't want me to touch you what's wrong with you Joey?

**Cate**   I'm not. You're cruel. I wouldn't shoot someone.

**Ian**   Pointed it at me.

**Cate**   Wouldn't shoot.

**Ian**   It's my job. I love this country. I won't see it destroyed by slag.

**Cate**   It's wrong to kill.

**Ian**   Planting bombs and killing little kiddies, that's wrong. That's what they do. Kids like your brother.

**Cate**   It's wrong.

**Ian**   Yes, it is.

**Cate**   No. You. Doing that.

**Ian**   When are you going to grow up?

**Cate**   I don't believe in killing.

**Ian**   You'll learn.

**Cate**   No I won't.

**Ian**   Can't always be taking it backing down letting them think they've got a right turn the other cheek SHIT some things are worth more than that have to be protected from shite.

**Cate**    I used to love you.

**Ian**    What's changed?

**Cate**    You.

**Ian**    No. Now you see me. That's all.

**Cate**    You're a nightmare.

*She shakes.*
**Ian** *watches a while, then hugs her.*
*She is still shaking so he hugs tightly to stop her.*

**Cate**    That hurts.

**Ian**    Sorry.

*He hugs her less tightly.*
*He has a coughing fit.*
*He spits into his handkerchief and waits for the pain to subside.*
*Then he lights a cigarette.*

**Ian**    How you feeling?

**Cate**    I ache.

**Ian**    (*Nods.*)

**Cate**    Everywhere.
I stink of you.

**Ian**    You want a bath?

**Cate** *begins to cough and retch.*
*She puts her fingers down her throat and produces a hair.*
*She holds it up and looks at* **Ian** *in disgust. She spits.*
**Ian** *goes into the bathroom and turns on one of the bath taps.*
**Cate** *stares out of the window.*
**Ian** *returns.*

**Cate**    Looks like there's a war on.

**Ian**   (*Doesn't look.*)

> Turning into Wogland.
> You coming to Leeds again?

**Cate**   Twenty-sixth.

**Ian**   Will you come and see me?

**Cate**   I'm going to the football.

*She goes to the bathroom.*
**Ian** *picks up the phone.*

**Ian**   Two English breakfasts, son.

*He finishes the remainder of the gin.*
**Cate** *returns.*

**Cate**   I can't piss. It's just blood.

**Ian**   Drink lots of water.

**Cate**   Or shit. It hurts.

**Ian**   It'll heal.

*There is a knock at the door. They both jump.*

**Cate**   DON'T ANSWER IT DON'T ANSWER IT
DON'T ANSWER IT

*She dives on the bed and puts her head under the pillow.*

**Ian**   Cate, shut up.

*He pulls the pillow off and puts the gun to her head.*

**Cate**   Do it. Go on, shoot me. Can't be no worse than what
you've done already. Shoot me if you want, then turn
it on yourself and do the world a favour.

**Ian**   (*Stares at her.*)

**Cate**   I'm not scared of you, Ian. Go on.

**Ian**   (*Gets off her.*)

**Cate**   (*Laughs.*)

**Ian**  Answer the door and suck the cunt's cock.

*Cate tries to open the door. It is locked.*
*Ian throws the key at her.*
*She opens the door.*
*The breakfasts are outside on a tray. She brings them in.*
*Ian locks the door.*
*Cate stares at the food.*

**Cate**  Sausages. Bacon.

**Ian**  Sorry. Forgot. Swap your meat for my tomatoes and mushrooms. And toast.

**Cate**  (*Begins to retch.*)

The smell.

*Ian takes a sausage off the plate and stuffs it in his mouth and keeps a rasher of bacon in his hand.*
*He puts the tray of food under the bed with a towel over it.*

**Ian**  Will you stay another day?

**Cate**  I'm having a bath and going home.

*She picks up her bag and goes into the bathroom, closing the door.*
*We hear the other bath tap being turned on.*
*There are two loud knocks at the outer door.*
*Ian draws his gun, goes to the door and listens.*
*The door is tried from outside. It is locked.*
*There are two more loud knocks.*

**Ian**  Who's there?

*Silence.*
*Then two more loud knocks.*

**Ian**  Who's there?

*Silence.*
*Then two more knocks.*
*Ian looks at the door.*
*Then he knocks twice.*
*Silence.*

*Then two more knocks from outside.*

**Ian** *thinks.*
*Then he knocks three times.*

*Silence.*
*Three knocks from outside.*

**Ian** *knocks once.*
*One knock from outside.*

**Ian** *knocks twice.*
*Two knocks.*

**Ian** *puts his gun back in the holster and unlocks the door.*

**Ian**   (*Under his breath.*) Speak the Queen's English fucking
   nigger.

*He opens the door.*
*Outside is a* **Soldier** *with a sniper's rifle.*
**Ian** *tries to push the door shut and draw his revolver.*
*The* **Soldier** *pushes the door open and takes* **Ian***'s gun*
*easily.*
*The two stand, both surprised, staring at each other.*
*Eventually.*

**Soldier**   What's that?

**Ian** *looks down and realises he is still holding a rasher of bacon.*

**Ian**   Pig.

*The* **Soldier** *holds out his hand.*
**Ian** *gives him the bacon and he eats it quickly, rind and all.*
*The* **Soldier** *wipes his mouth.*

**Soldier**   Got any more?

**Ian**   No.

**Soldier**   Got any more?

**Ian**   I –
   No.

**Soldier**   Got any more?

**Ian**  (*Points to the tray under the bed.*)

*The* **Soldier** *bends down carefully, never taking his eyes or rifle off*
**Ian**, *and takes the tray from under the bed.*
*He straightens up and glances down at the food.*

**Soldier**  Two.

**Ian**  I was hungry.

**Soldier**  I bet.

*The* **Soldier** *sits on the edge of the bed and very quickly devours both*
*breakfasts.*
*He sighs with relief and burps.*
*He nods towards the bathroom.*

**Soldier**  She in there?

**Ian**  Who?

**Soldier**  I can smell the sex.

(*He begins to search the room.*)

You a journalist?

**Ian**  I –

**Soldier**  Passport.

**Ian**  What for?

**Soldier**  (*Looks at him.*)

**Ian**  In the jacket.

*The* **Soldier** *is searching a chest of drawers.*
*He finds a pair of* **Cate**'s *knickers and holds them up.*

**Soldier**  Hers?

**Ian**  (*Doesn't answer.*)

**Soldier**  Or yours.

(*He closes his eyes and rubs them gently over his face, smelling*
*with pleasure.*)

What's she like?

**Ian**    (*Doesn't answer.*)

**Soldier**    Is she soft?
Is she – ?

**Ian**    (*Doesn't answer.*)

> *The* **Soldier** *puts* **Cate***'s knickers in his pocket and goes to the bathroom.*
> *He knocks on the door. No answer.*
> *He tries the door. It is locked.*
> *He forces it and goes in.*
> **Ian** *waits, in a panic.*
> *We hear the bath taps being turned off.*
> **Ian** *looks out of the window.*

**Ian**    Jesus Lord.

> *The* **Soldier** *returns.*

**Soldier**    Gone. Taking a risk. Lot of bastard soldiers out there.

> **Ian** *looks in the bathroom.* **Cate** *isn't there.*
> *The* **Soldier** *looks in* **Ian***'s jacket pockets and takes his keys, wallet and passport.*

**Soldier**    (*Looks at* **Ian***'s press card.*)

Ian Jones.
Journalist.

**Ian**    Oi.

**Soldier**    Oi.

> *They stare at each other.*

**Ian**    If you've come to shoot me –

**Soldier**    (*Reaches out to touch* **Ian***'s face but stops short of physical contact.*)

**Ian**   You taking the piss?

**Soldier**   Me?

(*He smiles.*)

Our town now.

(*He stands on the bed and urinates over the pillows.*)

**Ian** *is disgusted.*

*There is a blinding light, then a huge explosion.*

*Blackout.*

*The sound of summer rain.*


## Scene Three

*The hotel has been blasted by a mortar bomb.*

*There is a large hole in one of the walls, and everything is covered in dust which is still falling.*

*The **Soldier** is unconscious, rifle still in hand.*
*He has dropped **Ian**'s gun which lies between them.*

**Ian** *lies very still, eyes open.*

**Ian**   Mum?

*Silence.*
*The **Soldier** wakes and turns his eyes and rifle on **Ian** with the minimum possible movement.*
*He instinctively runs his free hand over his limbs and body to check that he is still in one piece. He is.*

**Soldier**   The drink.

**Ian** *looks around. There is a bottle of gin lying next to him with the lid off.*
*He holds it up to the light.*

**Ian**   Empty.

**Soldier**   (*Takes the bottle and drinks the last mouthful.*)

**Ian**   (*Chuckles.*)

Worse than me.

*The **Soldier** holds the bottle up and shakes it over his mouth, catching any remaining drops.*

*Ian finds his cigarettes in his shirt pocket and lights up.*

**Soldier**   Give us a cig.

**Ian**   Why?

**Soldier**   'Cause I've got a gun and you haven't.

*Ian considers the logic.*
*Then takes a single cigarette out of the packet and tosses it at the* **Soldier**.
*The **Soldier** picks up the cigarette and puts it in his mouth.*
*He looks at **Ian**, waiting for a light.*
*Ian holds out his cigarette.*
*The **Soldier** leans forward, touching the tip of his cigarette against the lit one, eyes always on **Ian**.*
*He smokes.*

**Soldier**   Never met an Englishman with a gun before, most of them don't know what a gun is. You a soldier?

**Ian**   Of sorts.

**Soldier**   Which side, if you can remember.

**Ian**   Don't know what the sides are here.
Don't know where . . .

(*He trails off confused, and looks at the **Soldier**.*)

Think I might be drunk.

**Soldier**   No. It's real.

(*He picks up the revolver and examines it.*)

Come to fight for us?

**Ian**   No, I –

**Soldier**   No, course not. English.

**Ian**   I'm Welsh.

**Soldier**   Sound English, fucking accent.

**Ian**   I live there.

**Soldier**   Foreigner?

**Ian**   English and Welsh is the same. British. I'm not an import.

**Soldier**   What's fucking Welsh, never heard of it.

**Ian**   Come over from God knows where have their kids and call them English they're not English born in England don't make you English.

**Soldier**   Welsh as in Wales?

**Ian**   It's attitude.

(*He turns away.*)

Look at the state of my fucking jacket. The bitch.

**Soldier**   Your girlfriend did that, angry was she?

**Ian**   She's not my girlfriend.

**Soldier**   What, then?

**Ian**   Mind your fucking own.

**Soldier**   Haven't been here long have you.

**Ian**   So?

**Soldier**   Learn some manners, Ian.

**Ian**   Don't call me that.

**Soldier**   What shall I call you?

**Ian**   Nothing.

*Silence.*

*The* **Soldier** *looks at* **Ian** *for a very long time, saying nothing.*
**Ian** *is uncomfortable.*
*Eventually.*

**Ian**   What?

**Soldier**   Nothing.

*Silence.*
**Ian** *is uneasy again.*

**Ian**   My name's Ian.

**Soldier**   I
Am
Dying to make love
Ian

**Ian**   (*Looks at him.*)

**Soldier**   You got a girlfriend?

**Ian**   (*Doesn't answer.*)

**Soldier**   I have.
Col.
Fucking beautiful.

**Ian**   Cate –

**Soldier**   Close my eyes and think about her.
She's –
She's –
She's –
She's –
She's –
She's –
She's –
When was the last time you – ?

**Ian**   (*Looks at him.*)

**Soldier**   When? I know it was recent, smell it, remember.

**Ian**   Last night. I think.

**Soldier**  Good?

**Ian**  Don't know. I was pissed. Probably not.

**Soldier**  Three of us –

**Ian**  Don't tell me.

**Soldier**  Went to a house just outside town. All gone. Apart from a small boy hiding in the corner. One of the others took him outside. Lay him on the ground and shot him through the legs. Heard crying in the basement. Went down. Three men and four women. Called the others. They held the men while I fucked the women. Youngest was twelve. Didn't cry, just lay there. Turned her over and –
Then she cried. Made her lick me clean. Closed my eyes and thought of –
Shot her father in the mouth. Brothers shouted. Hung them from the ceiling by their testicles.

**Ian**  Charming.

**Soldier**  Never done that?

**Ian**  No.

**Soldier**  Sure?

**Ian**  I wouldn't forget.

**Soldier**  You would.

**Ian**  Couldn't sleep with myself.

**Soldier**  What about your wife?

**Ian**  I'm divorced.

**Soldier**  Didn't you ever –

**Ian**  No.

**Soldier**  What about that girl locked herself in the bathroom.

**Ian**  (*Doesn't answer.*)

**Soldier**   Ah.

**Ian**   You did four in one go, I've only ever done one.

**Soldier**   You killed her?

**Ian**   (*Makes a move for his gun.*)

**Soldier**   Don't, I'll have to shoot you. Then I'd be lonely.

**Ian**   Course I haven't.

**Soldier**   Why not, don't seem to like her very much.

**Ian**   I do.
She's ... a woman.

**Soldier**   So?

**Ian**   I've never –
It's not –

**Soldier**   What?

**Ian**   (*Doesn't answer.*)

**Soldier**   Thought you were a soldier.

**Ian**   Not like that.

**Soldier**   Not like that, they're all like that.

**Ian**   My job –

**Soldier**   Even me. Have to be.
My girl –
Not going back to her. When I go back.
She's dead, see. Fucking bastard soldier, he –

*He stops.*
*Silence.*

**Ian**   I'm sorry.

**Soldier**   Why?

**Ian**   It's terrible.

**Soldier**   What is?

**Ian**    Losing someone, a woman, like that.

**Soldier**    You know, do you?

**Ian**    I –

**Soldier**    Like what?

**Ian**    Like –
You said –
A soldier –

**Soldier**    You're a soldier.

**Ian**    I haven't –

**Soldier**    What if you were ordered to?

**Ian**    Can't imagine it.

**Soldier**    Imagine it.

**Ian**    (*Imagines it.*)

**Soldier**    In the line of duty.
For your country.
Wales.

**Ian**    (*Imagines harder.*)

**Soldier**    Foreign slag.

**Ian**    (*Imagines harder. Looks sick.*)

**Soldier**    Would you?

**Ian**    (*Nods.*)

**Soldier**    How.

**Ian**    Quickly. Back of the head. Bam.

**Soldier**    That's all.

**Ian**    It's enough.

**Soldier**    You think?

**Ian**    Yes.

**Soldier**   You never killed anyone.

**Ian**   Fucking have.

**Soldier**   No.

**Ian**   Don't you fucking –

**Soldier**   Couldn't talk like this. You'd know.

**Ian**   Know what?

**Soldier**   Exactly. You don't know.

**Ian**   Know fucking what?

**Soldier**   Stay in the dark.

**Ian**   What? Fucking what? What don't I know?

**Soldier**   You think –

>    (*He stops and smiles.*)

>    I broke a woman's neck. Stabbed up between her
>    legs, on the fifth stab snapped her spine.

**Ian**   (*Looks sick.*)

**Soldier**   You couldn't do that.

**Ian**   No.

**Soldier**   You never killed.

**Ian**   Not like that.

**Soldier**   Not
Like
That

**Ian**   I'm not a torturer.

**Soldier**   You're close to them, gun to head. Tie them up, tell
them what you're going to do to them, make them
wait for it, then ... what?

**Ian**   Shoot them.

**Soldier**  You haven't got a clue.

**Ian**  What then?

**Soldier**  You never fucked a man before you killed him?

**Ian**  No.

**Soldier**  Or after?

**Ian**  Course not.

**Soldier**  Why not?

**Ian**  What for, I'm not queer.

**Soldier**  Col, they buggered her. Cut her throat. Hacked her ears and nose off, nailed them to the front door.

**Ian**  Enough.

**Soldier**  Ever seen anything like that?

**Ian**  Stop.

**Soldier**  Not in photos?

**Ian**  Never.

**Soldier**  Some journalist, that's your job.

**Ian**  What?

**Soldier**  Proving it happened. I'm here, got no choice. But you. You should be telling people.

**Ian**  No one's interested.

**Soldier**  You can do something, for me –

**Ian**  No.

**Soldier**  Course you can.

**Ian**  I can't do anything.

**Soldier**  Try.

**Ian**  I write ... stories. That's all. Stories. This isn't a story anyone wants to hear.

**Soldier**  Why not?

**Ian**  (*Takes one of the newspapers from the bed and reads.*)

'Kinky car dealer Richard Morris drove two teenage prostitutes into the country, tied them naked to fences and whipped them with a belt before having sex. Morris, from Sheffield, was jailed for three years for unlawful sexual intercourse with one of the girls, aged thirteen.'

(*He tosses the paper away.*)

Stories.

**Soldier**  Doing to them what they done to us, what good is that? At home I'm clean. Like it never happened. Tell them you saw me.
Tell them ... you saw me.

**Ian**  It's not my job.

**Soldier**  Whose is it?

**Ian**  I'm a home journalist, for Yorkshire. I don't cover foreign affairs.

**Soldier**  Foreign affairs, what you doing here?

**Ian**  I do other stuff. Shootings and rapes and kids getting fiddled by queer priests and schoolteachers. Not soldiers screwing each other for a patch of land. It has to be ... personal. Your girlfriend, she's a story. Soft and clean. Not you. Filthy, like the wogs. No joy in a story about blacks who gives a shit? Why bring you to light?

**Soldier**  You don't know fuck all about me.
I went to school.
I made love with Col.

Bastards killed her, now I'm here.
Now I'm here.

(*He pushes the rifle in* **Ian***'s face.*)

Turn over, Ian.

**Ian**   Why?

**Soldier**   Going to fuck you.

**Ian**   No.

**Soldier**   Kill you then.

**Ian**   Fine.

**Soldier**   See. Rather be shot than fucked and shot.

**Ian**   Yes.

**Soldier**   And now you agree with anything I say.

*He kisses* **Ian** *very tenderly on the lips.*
*They stare at each other.*

**Soldier**   You smell like her. Same cigarettes.

*The* **Soldier** *turns* **Ian** *over with one hand.*
*He holds the revolver to* **Ian***'s head with the other.*
*He pulls down* **Ian***'s trousers, undoes his own and rapes him – eyes
closed and smelling* **Ian***'s hair.*
*The* **Soldier** *is crying his heart out.*

**Ian***'s face registers pain but he is silent.*

*When the* **Soldier** *has finished he pulls up his trousers and pushes the
revolver up* **Ian***'s anus.*

**Soldier**   Bastard pulled the trigger on Col.
What's it like?

**Ian**   (*Tries to answer. He can't.*)

**Soldier**   (*Withdraws the gun and sits next to* **Ian***.*)

You never fucked by a man before?

**Ian**    (*Doesn't answer.*)

**Soldier**    Didn't think so. It's nothing. Saw thousands of
people packing into trucks like pigs trying to leave
town. Women threw their babies on board hoping
someone would look after them. Crushing each
other to death. Insides of people's heads came out
of their eyes. Saw a child most of his face blown off,
young girl I fucked hand up inside her trying to
claw my liquid out, starving man eating his dead
wife's leg. Gun was born here and won't die. Can't
get tragic about your arse. Don't think your Welsh
arse is different to any other arse I fucked. Sure you
haven't got any more food, I'm fucking starving.

**Ian**    Are you going to kill me?

**Soldier**    Always covering your own arse.

*The* **Soldier** *grips* **Ian**'s *head in his hands.*

*He puts his mouth over one of* **Ian**'s *eyes, sucks it out, bites it off and
eats it.*

*He does the same to the other eye.*

**Soldier**    He ate her eyes.
Poor bastard.
Poor love.
Poor fucking bastard.

*Blackout.*

*The sound of autumn rain.*


**Scene Four**

*The same.*

*The* **Soldier** *lies close to* **Ian**, *the revolver in his hand.*
*He has blown his own brain out.*

**Cate** *enters through the bathroom door, soaking wet and carrying a baby.*
*She steps over the* **Soldier** *with a glance.*
*Then she sees* **Ian**.

**Cate**   You're a nightmare.

**Ian**   Cate?

**Cate**   It won't stop.

**Ian**   Catie? You here?

**Cate**   Everyone in town is crying.

**Ian**   Touch me.

**Cate**   Soldiers have taken over.

**Ian**   They've won?

**Cate**   Most people gave up.

**Ian**   You seen Matthew?

**Cate**   No.

**Ian**   Will you tell him for me?

**Cate**   He isn't here.

**Ian**   Tell him –
Tell him –

**Cate**   No.

**Ian**   Don't know what to tell him.
I'm cold.
Tell him –
You here?

**Cate**   A woman gave me her baby.

**Ian**   You come for me, Catie? Punish me or rescue me makes no difference I love you Cate tell him for me do it for me touch me Cate.

**Cate**   Don't know what to do with it.

**Ian**  I'm cold.

**Cate**  Keeps crying.

**Ian**  Tell him –

**Cate**  I CAN'T.

**Ian**  Will you stay with me, Cate?

**Cate**  No.

**Ian**  Why not?

**Cate**  I have to go back soon.

**Ian**  Shaun know what we did?

**Cate**  No.

**Ian**  Better tell him.

**Cate**  No.

**Ian**  He'll know. Even if you don't.

**Cate**  How?

**Ian**  Smell it. Soiled goods. Don't want it, not when you can have someone clean.

**Cate**  What's happened to your eyes?

**Ian**  I need you to stay, Cate. Won't be for long.

**Cate**  Do you know about babies?

**Ian**  No.

**Cate**  What about Matthew?

**Ian**  He's twenty-four.

**Cate**  When he was born.

**Ian**  They shit and cry. Hopeless.

**Cate**  Bleeding.

**Ian**  Will you touch me?

**Cate**  No.

**Ian**  So I know you're here.

**Cate**  You can hear me.

**Ian**  Won't hurt you, I promise.

**Cate**  (*Goes to him slowly and touches the top of his head.*)

**Ian**  Help me.

**Cate**  (*Strokes his hair.*)

**Ian**  Be dead soon anyway, Cate.
And it hurts.
Help me to –
Help me –
Finish
It

**Cate**  (*Withdraws her hand.*)

**Ian**  Catie?

**Cate**  Got to get something for Baby to eat.

**Ian**  Won't find anything.

**Cate**  May as well look.

**Ian**  Fucking bastards ate it all.

**Cate**  It'll die.

**Ian**  Needs its mother's milk.

**Cate**  Ian.

**Ian**  Stay.
Nowhere to go, where are you going to go?
Bloody dangerous on your own, look at me.
Safer here with me.

**Cate** *considers.*
*Then sits down with the baby some distance from* **Ian**.
*He relaxes when he hears her sit.*

**Cate** *rocks the baby.*

**Ian**   Not as bad as all that, am I?

**Cate**   (*Looks at him.*)

**Ian**   Will you help me, Catie?

**Cate**   How.

**Ian**   Find my gun?

> **Cate** *thinks.*
> *Then gets up and searches around, baby in arms.*
> *She sees the revolver in the* **Soldier***'s hand and stares at it for some time.*

**Ian**   Found it?

**Cate**   No.

> *She takes the revolver from the* **Soldier** *and fiddles with it.*
> *It springs open and she stares in at the bullets.*
> *She removes them and closes the gun.*

**Ian**   That it?

**Cate**   Yes.

**Ian**   Can I have it?

**Cate**   I don't think so.

**Ian**   Catie.

**Cate**   What?

**Ian**   Come on.

**Cate**   Don't tell me what to do.

**Ian**   I'm not, love. Can you keep that baby quiet.

**Cate**   It's not doing anything. It's hungry.

**Ian**   We're all bloody hungry, don't shoot myself I'll starve to death.

**Cate**   It's wrong to kill yourself.

**Ian**   No it's not.

**Cate**   God wouldn't like it.

**Ian**   There isn't one.

**Cate**   How do you know?

**Ian**   No God. No Father Christmas. No fairies. No Narnia. No fucking nothing.

**Cate**   Got to be something.

**Ian**   Why?

**Cate**   Doesn't make sense otherwise.

**Ian**   Don't be fucking stupid, doesn't make sense anyway. No reason for there to be a God just because it would be better if there was.

**Cate**   Thought you didn't want to die.

**Ian**   I can't see.

**Cate**   My brother's got blind friends. You can't give up.

**Ian**   Why not?

**Cate**   It's weak.

**Ian**   I know you want to punish me, trying to make me live.

**Cate**   I don't.

**Ian**   Course you fucking do, I would. There's people I'd love to suffer but they don't, they die and that's it.

**Cate**   What if you're wrong?

**Ian**   I'm not.

**Cate**   But if.

**Ian**   I've seen dead people. They're dead. They're not somewhere else, they're dead.

**Cate**   What about people who've seen ghosts?

**Ian**  What about them? Imagining it. Or making it up or
wishing the person was still alive.

**Cate**  People who've died and come back say they've seen
tunnels and lights –

**Ian**  Can't die and come back. That's not dying, it's fainting.
When you die, it's the end.

**Cate**  I believe in God.

**Ian**  Everything's got a scientific explanation.

**Cate**  No.

**Ian**  Give me my gun.

**Cate**  What are you going to do?

**Ian**  I won't hurt you.

**Cate**  I know.

**Ian**  End it.
Got to, Cate, I'm ill.
Just speeding it up a bit.

**Cate**  (*Thinks hard.*)

**Ian**  Please.

**Cate**  (*Gives him the gun.*)

**Ian**  (*Takes the gun and puts it in his mouth.
He takes it out again.*)

Don't stand behind me.

*He puts the gun back in his mouth.
He pulls the trigger. The gun clicks, empty.
He shoots again. And again and again and again.
He takes the gun out of his mouth.*

**Ian**  Fuck.

**Cate**    Fate, see. You're not meant to do it. God –

**Ian**    The cunt.

*(He throws the gun away in despair.)*

**Cate**    *(Rocks the baby and looks down at it.)*

Oh no.

**Ian**    What.

**Cate**    It's dead.

**Ian**    Lucky bastard.

**Cate**    *(Bursts out laughing, unnaturally, hysterically, uncontrollably. She laughs and laughs and laughs and laughs and laughs.)*

*Blackout.*

*The sound of heavy winter rain.*


## Scene Five

*The same.*

**Cate** *is burying the baby under the floor.*

*She looks around and finds two pieces of wood.*
*She rips the lining out of* **Ian***'s jacket and binds the wood together in a cross which she sticks into the floor.*
*She collects a few of the scattered flowers and places them under the cross.*

**Cate**    I don't know her name.

**Ian**    Don't matter. No one's going to visit.

**Cate**    I was supposed to look after her.

**Ian**    Can bury me next to her soon. Dance on my grave.

**Cate**    Don't feel no pain or know nothing you shouldn't know –

**Ian**    Cate?

**Cate**   Shh.

**Ian**   What you doing?

**Cate**   Praying. Just in case.

**Ian**   Will you pray for me?

**Cate**   No.

**Ian**   When I'm dead, not now.

**Cate**   No point when you're dead.

**Ian**   You're praying for her.

**Cate**   She's baby.

**Ian**   So?

**Cate**   Innocent.

**Ian**   Can't you forgive me?

**Cate**   Don't see bad things or go bad places –

**Ian**   She's dead, Cate.

**Cate**   Or meet anyone who'll do bad things.

**Ian**   She won't, Cate, she's dead.

**Cate**   Amen.

   (*She starts to leave.*)

**Ian**   Where you going?

**Cate**   I'm hungry.

**Ian**   Cate, it's dangerous. There's no food.

**Cate**   Can get some off a soldier.

**Ian**   How?

**Cate**   (*Doesn't answer.*)

**Ian**   Don't do that.

**Cate**   Why not?

**Ian**    That's not you.

**Cate**    I'm hungry.

**Ian**    I know so am I.
But.
I'd rather –
It's not –
Please, Cate.
I'm blind.

**Cate**    I'm hungry.

(*She goes.*)

**Ian**    Cate? Catie?
If you get some food –
Fuck.

*Darkness.*
*Light.*

**Ian** *masturbating.*

**Ian**    cunt cunt cunt cunt cunt cunt cunt cunt cunt cunt cunt

*Darkness.*
*Light.*

**Ian** *strangling himself with his bare hands.*

*Darkness.*
*Light.*

**Ian** *shitting.*
*And then trying to clean it up with newspaper.*

*Darkness.*
*Light.*

**Ian** *laughing hysterically.*

*Darkness.*
*Light.*

**Ian** *having a nightmare.*

*Darkness.*
*Light.*

**Ian** *crying, huge bloody tears.*
*He is hugging the* **Soldier**'s *body for comfort.*

*Darkness.*
*Light.*

**Ian** *lying very still, weak with hunger.*

*Darkness.*
*Light.*

**Ian** *tears the cross out of the ground, rips up the floor and lifts the baby's body out.*

*He eats the baby.*

*He puts the remains back in the baby's blanket and puts the bundle back in the hole.*
*A beat, then he climbs in after it and lies down, head poking out of the floor.*

*He dies with relief.*

*It starts to rain on him, coming through the roof.*

*Eventually.*

**Ian**    Shit.

**Cate** *enters carrying some bread, a large sausage and a bottle of gin. There is blood seeping from between her legs.*

**Cate**    You're sitting under a hole.

**Ian**    I know.

**Cate**    Get wet.

**Ian**    Aye.

**Cate**    Stupid bastard.

*She pulls a sheet off the bed and wraps it around her.*

*She sits next to* **Ian***'s head.*

*She eats her fill of the sausage and bread, then washes it down with gin.*

**Ian** *listens.*

*She feeds* **Ian** *with the remaining food.*

*She pours gin in* **Ian***'s mouth.*

*She finishes feeding* **Ian** *and sits apart from him, huddled for warmth.*

*She drinks the gin.*
*She sucks her thumb.*

*Silence.*

*It rains.*

**Ian**    Thank you.

*Blackout.*